P9-CEV-952

GRIZZLY BEARS
WILD AND STRONG

Norman Pearl

PowerKiDS
press.

New York

Published in 2009 by The Rosen Publishing Group, Inc.
29 East 21st Street, New York, NY 10010

First Edition

Editor: Amelie von Zumbusch
Book Design: Julio Gil
Photo Researcher: Jessica Gerweck

Photo Credits: Cover, pp. 5, 7, 9, 11, 17, 21 Shutterstock.com; p. 13 © Alan & Sandy Carey/Peter Arnold Inc.; p. 15 © STOUFFER PRODUCTIONS/Animals Animals; p. 19 © Getty Images; back cover (top to bottom) Shutterstock.com, Shutterstock.com, © Kim Wolhuter/Getty Images, Shutterstock.com, © Stephen Frink/Getty Images, Shutterstock.com.

Library of Congress Cataloging-in-Publication Data

Pearl, Norman.
  Grizzly bears : wild and strong / Norman Pearl. — 1st ed.
      p. cm. — (Powerful predators)
  Includes index.
  ISBN 978-1-4042-4506-8 (library binding)
  1. Grizzly bear—Juvenile literature. I. Title.
  QL737.C27P367 2009
  599.784—dc22
                                                    2007049960

Manufactured in the United States of America

Contents

Great Fishing Here!

Some of the greatest fishing spots in North America have no fishermen. Instead, dozens of bears stand in the water. They catch fish with their claws and mouths. These big animals are known as grizzly bears.

Grizzly bear is the name commonly used for North American brown bears. Brown bears are a species, or kind, of bear. Though most of North America's brown bears are called grizzly bears, brown bears living near the Pacific Ocean are also sometimes just called brown bears. Brown bears from Alaska's Kodiak Island are called Kodiak bears. Whatever they are called, these bears are skilled hunters with sharp senses and powerful claws.

Brooks Falls, in Alaska's Katmai National Park, is a favorite fishing spot for grizzly bears.

Meet the Grizzly Bear

Most grizzly bears are brown, but some are nearly black or even cream colored. Some bears have fur that is tipped with gray, or grizzled. That is why they are called grizzly bears.

Grizzlies, as these bears are sometimes called, are huge. A **male** grizzly generally weighs about 500 pounds (227 kg), while **females** weigh around 375 pounds (170 kg). When these bears stand up, they are between 6 and 7 feet (1.8–2.1 m) tall. This is taller than most people. Grizzly bears are stronger than people, too. These bears have large paws with long, **curved** claws. It is not safe to get close to a grizzly!

All grizzly bears have shoulder humps. Looking for a shoulder hump is one of the easiest ways to tell if a bear is a grizzly.

Stay Away from the Bear!

Camping and **hiking** are fun, but meeting up with a grizzly is not. These strong bears can hurt people badly. You should be very careful around grizzlies. Try these tips to stay safe in grizzly country:

- When camping, do not leave food out. The smell can draw a grizzly to your camp.
- Try not to surprise a grizzly. Let grizzly bears know you are there. Talk loudly and make noise as you walk through the woods.
- Never run from a grizzly. These bears are faster than people. Grizzly bears can run as fast as 35 miles per hour (56 km/h).

Since grizzly bears are so fast, you should never run from a grizzly. Instead, try not to panic and back away slowly.

Let's Eat!

Though grizzly bears are strong enough to hurt people, these bears do not often **attack** people. People are not grizzly-bear food. Grizzlies eat lots of other things, though. These bears are **omnivorous**. That means that they eat both plants and animals.

Grizzlies eat bugs, roots, plant **bulbs**, and berries. Sometimes, grizzlies **prey** on large animals, such as **elk**, moose, mountain goats, and sheep. More often, they eat fish, mice, rats, and carrion. Carrion is the rotting remains of a dead animal. Grizzlies have a great sense of smell. They can smell a dead animal from miles (km) away.

Salmon is an important food for some grizzly bears. Grizzlies often catch salmon when the fish swim up rivers to lay their eggs.

Life as a Grizzly

Grizzlies generally rest during the day and look for food in the mornings and evenings. Finding food is very important to these bears. Grizzly bears will attack other animals or people that get close to their food.

Food becomes even more important in the summer and fall. Then, grizzly bears may eat as much as 80 to 90 pounds (36–40 kg) of food a day. They need to put on weight to build up their stores of fat. This fat stores **energy**, which the bears will need to keep them alive through the long winter ahead.

Grizzly bears that live inland eat mostly berries, nuts, and small animals, while bears living nearer to the coast eat lots of fish.

A Long Winter Nap

Grizzly bears spend the winter in a deep sleep in their dens. A grizzly's den may be a cave or a hole in a dead tree. Some grizzlies build their own dens. They dig large holes in the ground with their long, strong claws.

Grizzlies use up most of the energy stored in their body fat while they are sleeping. When the bears leave their dens in the spring, they are very hungry. The hungriest bears are female grizzlies with babies. Mother grizzly bears give birth to babies in their winter dens. The babies drink their mothers' milk, using up even more of her stored fat.

Each winter, grizzly bears spend between four and seven months asleep in their dens.

Cute Cubs

Young grizzlies are called cubs. Grizzly cubs are generally born in January or February. Grizzly mothers most often have two cubs at a time. Cubs are helpless at birth. They have no teeth and almost no hair. Their eyes are closed, and the cubs cannot see. Newborn cubs curl up next to their mothers and drink their milk.

Grizzly cubs grow quickly. When they are about one month old, their eyes open. At about one year old, cubs can climb trees. Grizzly cubs stay with their mothers for two to three years. Then, the large, young bears go off on their own.

Grizzly bear cubs are interested in the world around them. They like to play, climb, and learn new things.

Which Bear Is the Biggest?

Though all grown brown bears are big, the world's largest brown bears are the Kodiak bears. A male Kodiak bear is about 10 feet (3 m) tall when it stands up. Even on all fours, this bear is about 5 feet (1.5 m) tall. That is taller than most fifth graders! Female bears are smaller but still big.

There are about 3,000 Kodiak bears. These bears have lived on Kodiak Island, in Alaska, for 12,000 years. In time, the bears on Kodiak Island became larger than the bears on the mainland. Today, many **scientists** believe Kodiak bears are a special **subspecies** of brown bear.

Large male Kodiak bears often weigh as much as 1,500 pounds (680 kg).
Scientists believe they are the largest omnivores that live on land.

Where the Bears Are

Kodiak bears are found only on Kodiak Island. Grizzlies are found in both Canada and the United States. In the United States, grizzlies may be spotted in Alaska, Wyoming, Montana, Idaho, and Washington. There are many grizzlies in Yellowstone National Park.

Years ago, grizzlies were common in many more places. The bears could be found as far south as Mexico and as far east as Iowa. California is thought to have been home to 10,000 grizzlies. However, people now live and work on the land where grizzlies once lived. These bears can now only be found in a few wild places, such as mountains and forests.

Scientists think that there are now more than 500 grizzly bears
in and around Yellowstone National Park, where this bear lives.

What's Ahead for the Grizzly?

Today, grizzly bears have far fewer places to live than they used to. There were once about 50,000 grizzlies in North America. Today, less than 1,200 are left in the lower 48 states. These are the states below Alaska and east of Hawaii.

In 1975, laws were passed to keep the grizzly bear safe in the lower 48 states. Things got better, but there are still very few grizzlies. We will have to work hard to keep grizzly bears and the places they live safe if we want these strong, wild animals to be here in the years to come.

Glossary

attack (uh-TAK) To start a fight with.

bulbs (BULBZ) Underground plant parts from which some plants grow.

curved (KURVD) Having a shape that bends or curls.

elk (ELK) A very large kind of deer.

energy (EH-nur-jee) The power to work or to act.

females (FEE-maylz) Women and girls.

hiking (HY-king) Taking a long walk.

male (MAYL) Having to do with men and boys.

omnivorous (om-NIV-rus) Eating both plants and animals.

prey (PRAY) To hunt for food.

scientists (SY-un-tists) People who study the world.

subspecies (SUB-spee-sheez) A different kind of the same animal.

Index

A
animals, 4, 10, 22

C
camping, 8

claws, 4, 6, 14

E
elk, 10

energy, 12, 14

F
females, 6

fish, 4, 10

fishermen, 4

fur, 6

H
hunters, 4

K
Kodiak Island, 4, 18, 20

M
mouths, 4

N
North America, 4, 22

P
Pacific Ocean, 4

paws, 6

people, 8, 10, 12, 20

plant bulbs, 10

S
scientists, 18

sense(s), 4, 10

species, 4

subspecies, 18

W
water, 4

Web Sites

Due to the changing nature of Internet links, PowerKids Press has developed an online list of Web sites related to the subject of this book. This site is updated regularly. Please use this link to access the list:

www.powerkidslinks.com/pred/grizzly/